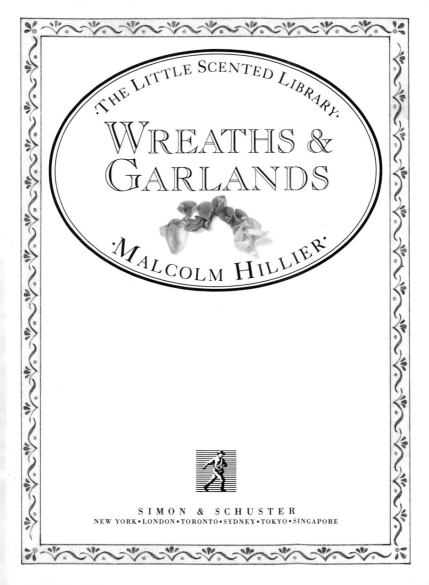

·THE LITTLE SCENTED LIBRARY·

WREATHS & GARLANDS

·MALCOLM HILLIER·

SIMON & SCHUSTER
NEW YORK•LONDON•TORONTO•SYDNEY•TOKYO•SINGAPORE

A DORLING KINDERSLEY BOOK

SIMON & SCHUSTER
SIMON & SCHUSTER BUILDING, ROCKEFELLER CENTER
1230 AVENUE OF THE AMERICAS, NEW YORK, NY 10020

FIRST PUBLISHED IN GREAT BRITAIN IN 1992
BY DORLING KINDERSLEY LIMITED,
9 HENRIETTA STREET, LONDON WC2E 8PS
PRINTED IN HONG KONG
10 9 8 7 6 5 4 3 2 1

LIBRARY OF CONGRESS CATALOGING-IN-PUBLICATION DATA
IS AVAILABLE ON REQUEST

INCLUDES INDEX

2

CONTENTS

INTRODUCTION

GARLANDS, WREATHS, and swags are magnificent decorations for festive seasons and lavish celebrations. They look fabulous festooning the side of a table, or adorning a simple doorway, and can be wound around poles in a tent, or circle a wedding cake. I always think that a garland is at its loveliest when it is decorating a staircase. As guests inadvertently brush past the garland, the scents of the flowers and foliage are released, filling the air with a heavenly fragrance.

Throughout history, we have bound together flowers and foliage to make fragrant wreaths and garlands. The Ancient Greeks and Romans made rings of sweet bay and laurel, which were worn by conquering heroes and kings. In the Far East and the Oceanic islands, it has always been traditional to string bright flowers together in a loop to present as a gift to visitors.

Whatever the occasion, whether it is a wedding, a Christmas party, or an anniversary, a sumptuous garland or an exuberant swag of fresh flowers and foliage is certain to fill the room with heavenly scents and lend a festive air to the celebrations.

SPRING FLOWERS

*D*ELICIOUS SCENTS and fresh, clear colors herald the start of spring after the long, cold winter months. There are so many truly glorious spring flowers, and although they are generally not as long lasting as summer blooms, their fragile beauty looks quite wonderful in wreaths and garlands. The longer-lasting varieties are broom, cyclamen, hyacinths, tulips, wattle, and mimosa. Other spring flowers can be used in wreaths and garlands, but they do require cool conditions.

Wattle *is long lasting and has a sweet, honeyed fragrance when fresh or dried.*

Grape hyacinth *is beautiful used in wedding circlets and headdresses.*

Narcissus *can be intensely perfumed, especially those related to the Jonquil variety.*

Lilac *has a heady scent and blooms in late spring. The flowers can also be white, cream, or pink.*

Tulip has a warm, peppery scent and lasts well when used in both garlands and wreaths.

Broom, with its feathery sprays, gives an informal look to any wreath or garland.

Lily-of-the-valley is exquisite used in headdresses and small, delicate garlands.

Polyanthus and auricula have very fragrant, colorful, and decorative flowers. They prefer cool conditions.

Cyclamen is fairly long lasting. The Persian varieties are particularly sweetly scented.

Cherry blossom has a sweet, delicate scent and flowers that are evocative of the beginning of the spring season.

Hyacinth, with its pervasive perfume, has a large bloom and so is best cut and wired as single flowers.

SUMMER FLOWERS

*S*OME OF THE MOST EXQUISITE and highly scented flowers are those that are available in the summer months. Roses, pinks, carnations, lilies, and freesias are among the best summer flowers for garlands, as they are the most long lasting.

Honeysuckle *has a sweet scent redolent of nutmeg.*

Rose 'Norwich Castle' *flowers profusely and has a subtle fragrance.*

Sage *has attractive, aromatic leaves.*

Stephanotis *is highly fragrant and is very suitable for a wedding garland.*

Rose 'The Alchemist' *is highly scented.*

Lilies *have a rich, spicy fragrance and are excellent flowers for larger garlands.*

Lavender is often used in garlands for its unique scent.

Peony has a sweet, buttery scent.

Star jasmine has a strong, sweet fragrance.

Carnation has a perfume reminiscent of cloves.

9

Freesia has a clear, sweet perfume.

Rosa glauca is not highly scented, but has very attractive foliage.

Scented geranium has fragrant, lemony leaves. Its attractive foliage is good in garlands.

Pinks are very sweet smelling and are also long lasting.

MAKING A GARLAND

*G*ARLANDS are usually
made by attaching
individual flowers
or small bunches to a length
of rope, cord, or wire. It is a
fairly slow, time-consuming
process, so to save time you
can make up some bunches
of flowers and soak them in
a bucket of water, or even
in the bath, overnight, and
assemble the garland the
following day. To hang your

display, wrap some reel
wire around the ends of the
swag or garland and make a
tight loop at each end. You
can then hook the garland
around some small nails or
strong brass tacks, that have
been inserted into the
banister rail, window frame,
tent pole, or table.

1 Prepare little bunches of
conditioned flowers. Lay one
bunch over the end of a length of
rope or wire and attach it with
three twists of reel wire,
so it overlaps
the end.

2 Take the wire behind the bunch, and continue to tie in the bunches until the length of rope or wire is covered. Wind in strands of decorative foliage, such as trailing smilax, to add greenery and soften the edges. After the bunches are all attached, you can tuck additional flowers into the garland quite easily if required.

PEONY SWAG
Rosemary, peonies, pinks, and lavender combine to create a textured, thick, and pleasantly aromatic swag.

SUMMER WREATHS

APTURE the heady scents of summer in a fragrant, fresh flower wreath. There is a tremendous variety of spectacular flowers available in the summer months, many of which are extremely perfumed and fairly long lasting. A decorative wreath of fresh summer flowers, finished with a bright bow, will lend an exuberant air to any festivities. If you are making a garland or wreath for a particular occasion, you may like to choose a color theme that is appropriate to the celebration. This wreath, for example, would be ideal for a golden wedding anniversary.

13

GOLDEN WREATH

*This cheery wreath
exudes an intensely
sweet, summer scent.
It contains a range
of long-lasting flowers
and foliage: carnations;
roses; fennel; golden privet; lilies;
freesias; and bells of Ireland. Notice
how the lime green of the bells of
Ireland acts as a startling contrast
to the yellows and oranges of all the other
flowers, and brings this festive wreath to life.*

SPRING GARLANDS

O F ALL THE SEASONS in the year, spring is probably the most exciting. It is the season of rejuvenation, and our spirits are raised by the freshness in the air and the new growth that surrounds us. As a result, spring is a natural time to celebrate. There are so many glorious spring flowers, and there is really nothing lovelier or more festive than a window, doorway, table, or staircase garlanded with fragrant fresh spring flowers and foliage for that special celebration.

EASTER GARLAND

Small bunches of bright, golden polyanthuses and yellow ranunculi are mixed with pale pink cherry blossom, white lilac, and ice pink broom in this sunny Easter garland. The flowers are attached in bunches to a length of fine rope ¼in (6mm) thick (see pages 10-11), and are interwoven with sprays of asparagus foliage.

FLORAL HEADDRESSES

*T*HE WEDDING CEREMONY is one of the most memorable occasions of our lives. It is hard to imagine the celebration without flowers, as they add so much to the magical atmosphere of the day. The bride and her bridesmaids may carry posies of flowers, and pretty blossoms decorate their hair.

COUNTRY GARLAND
This simple but pretty headdress contains small bunches of ice pink broom mixed with deep blue hyacinths and clear green bells of Ireland. It has a soft, pure fragrance and long-lasting beauty. The base of this headdress is made from an 18-gauge wire covered in some stem tape. The flowers are attached to the wire, and this is curved into shape to make an attractive circlet.

SUMMER CIRCLET

Miniature cream roses, spicy picotee carnations, cream and orange roses, spikes of honey-scented broom, highly perfumed tuberoses, and huckleberry foliage are attached to a base of pussy willow stems to make this garland. The flowers last well, so the circlet can be made up to twelve hours in advance.

WEDDING CIRCLETS

HESE DELIGHTFUL wedding circlets make an unusual alternative to a more formal bride's or bridesmaid's bouquet. You can make them in the same way as a garland (see pages 10–11), but if you prefer, you could use an attractive base of twigs or vine to achieve a more rustic effect.

BRIDE'S CIRCLET
Mignonette, delicate white spray roses, and pink and white lilies are attached to a fairly stout vine base to make this fragrant wedding circlet. It is traditional for the bride to wear or carry "something blue," so I have also included willow gentian for good luck. The lilies and roses are long lasting and can be attached twelve hours in advance, whereas the mignonette needs to be bound in at the very last moment.

BRIDESMAID'S CIRCLET

*Small children love to carry a circlet of flowers.
This can be attached to a child's wrist, so that
even the youngest bridesmaid will not drop or
lose her flowers during the wedding ceremony.
In this circlet I have set tiny green orchids,
bright, sunny African marigolds, delicate
yellow rosebuds, and pale and deep salmon
pinks against a background of dark green
smilax. I have not completely covered the base
with flowers and foliage, as I think it is quite
pretty to allow the twigs to show through.*

DELICATE GARLANDS

*F*OR A SPECIAL CELEBRATION, create a delicate garland to surround a wedding cake, wrap around a tent pole, or edge a buffet table. The delicate leaves of the climber, smilax, make a perfect background, and freesias, carnations, and smaller varieties of spray roses are particularly suitable for a finer rope.

FRAGRANT FLOURISH
I have combined the delicate, muted colors of lilac freesias with peach roses, cream frilled carnations, and lagurus grass against a background of smilax.

21

SPICY SCENTS

*A*ROMATIC SPICES from the East have been used to perfume our clothes and rooms since the days of the Ancient Egyptians. We place small scented sachets of spices in drawers to keep our clothes and linens fragrant and fresh, and we hang pretty pomanders in our wardrobes to exude the musky scent of cloves. A decorative wreath or garland covered in aromatic spices is an excellent way of filling even a large room with a delicious, warm, exotic perfume. It would be wonderful in either a living or dining room.

SPICE WREATH

This fragrant, heart-shaped spice wreath is made from a tube of chicken wire filled with dried sphagnum moss (see pages 24-25). Make sure that the moss is completely dry and firmly packed into the chicken-wire frame, as it is going to have to carry the weight of the pomanders. Bend the moss-filled tube into a heart shape, and bind the ends together with 23-gauge wire. Next, attach overlapping bunches of dried oregano to cover the frame, and then add the spices. Citrus pomanders, small bags filled with fragrant ground spices, and bundles of cinnamon can be wired into the wreath; other decorative seeds, such as poppy heads and cedar cones, can be pushed or glued into place.

MAKING A SWAG

*F*RAGRANT swags look best over a window, door, or painting. A swag should have plenty of curving movement so it looks as if it has been looped and tied back at the sides.

24

1 Make a tube by rolling damp sphagnum moss in a piece of chicken wire 12in (30cm) wide and as long as you need.

FESTIVE WINTER SWAG

This thick, aromatic swag is very striking and is surprisingly easy to make. Tangy eucalyptus sprigs and fragrant conifer are used to fill in a framework of moss, then clusters of red cotoneaster berries and three large shells are added to embellish the whole. Draped over a mantelpiece, mirror, or door, this handsome evergreen swag would make a suitably festive autumn or winter decoration.

2 Using mossing wire, bind bunches of plant material to the frame so that they overlap and conceal the chicken wire.

CELEBRATION FLOWERS

*F*LOWERS MAKE THE PERFECT GIFT for birthdays, wedding anniversaries, Mother's Day, and any other special occasion that your family and friends may celebrate. Whether you tie the flowers in a pretty bouquet or posy, fill elegant cornucopias with beautiful blooms, make up a window box display of bright, freshly gathered spring flowers, or fill a basket with dried flowers and bunches of fragrant herbs, your gift will always be greatly appreciated and warmly received.

SPRING ANNIVERSARY BASKET

This colorful basket of flowers looks splendid hanging on the wall, and will last for up to a week in cool conditions. To make the unusual window box-style container, I soaked two wet foam blocks in water and covered them in plastic to prevent any drips. I then formed a flat sandwich of chicken wire filled with dried sphagnum moss and wrapped it securely around the two blocks of foam. To conceal the sides and base of the "box," I glued some eucalyptus leaves onto the chicken-wire frame. I chose to fill the basket with some hyacinths, grape hyacinths, willow gentian, tulips, and narcissi. Finally, I completely covered the area around the base of the stems with sphagnum moss.

LOOPED FESTOONS

*L*OOPED SWAGS, OR FESTOONS, are best seen when hanging on walls, around a doorway, above a window, or across the front of a large buffet table. They are particularly festive and are splendid for parties or lavish celebrations of all kinds.

   If you are making a large swag, it is best to work with small, manageable lengths of garlanding, which can be made up separately and then joined together with wire, rather than one long rope, which can be unwieldy. Choose flowers and leaves that will last for several hours out of water. Fortunately, there are many of these. Scented roses, chrysanthemums, carnations, pinks, and freesias, as well as lilies, should all survive for twelve hours or more if they are in peak condition.

OPULENT SWAG
Here the scented roses
'Parfuma', 'Nicole',
and 'Baccarola' are
interlaced with sprigs
of asparagus fern and
hypericum seed heads.
A wire frame, filled
with moss, supports the
weight of the larger and
heavier flowers.

FRAGRANT HANGINGS

*F*RAGRANT HANGINGS made from a variety of
dried plant materials look
stunning on the walls
of the kitchen or hall. They
are quite unique and can
be every bit as beautiful
as a painting. Let your
imagination run riot,
and create a striking
and unconventional
plaque of your own!

MOSS TREES

*This cluster of trees makes
an unusual and fragrant
hanging. To construct the
plaque, I made a frame from
three vertical pieces of birch
bough screwed firmly onto a
long, horizontal, wooden baton.
I then constructed three circular bases
for the tree tops. These were made from
two disks of chicken wire stuffed with dried
sphagnum moss (see pages 24-25), and stitched firmly
together with 23-gauge wire. Next, I stapled the tree tops
onto the frame, overlapping the edges, and covered them
with pieces of fragrant oakmoss, glued on to
resemble foliage. I chose to decorate the trees
with pretty rose-shaped cones, mock crab
apples, berries, and wired pecan nuts,
but there is a large variety of other
dried and artificial plant materials
that you could use if you prefer.*

BAY WREATHS

THE ANCIENT GREEKS and Romans crowned their heroes with bay wreaths and garlands. Today, we can use this piquant herb to make aromatic decorations for our walls. The intense green of the fresh leaves will fade as they dry, but a bay wreath should retain its beauty for many months.

CIRCULAR WREATH

To make this wreath, I glued bay leaves onto a moss-filled, chicken-wire frame. I then attached bunches of thyme and rosemary, which I tied with raffia bows.

TRADITIONAL WREATH
*Bright scarlet chilis and fresh limes
add an unusual, colorful touch
to this otherwise traditional
wreath. Chilis will retain
much of their red color
when they are dried,
whereas limes tend
to turn brown. You
could use a citrus
pomander as an
alternative to
fresh limes if
you prefer.*

AUTUMN WREATHS

*A*UTUMN IS A TIME of soft colors and warm, mellow scents. The pure, sweet perfume of the late-flowering roses and the sharp tang of the few remaining chrysanthemums mingle with the pervasive aroma of harvesting and bonfires, as our gardens are tidied before the onset of winter. Capture the flavor of autumn with a seasonal wreath made from dried flowers, herbs, and bundles of corn.

THANKSGIVING WREATH

This rustic wreath would be very decorative hanging on the front door for Harvest festival or Thanksgiving celebrations. To make the wreath, I constructed a frame of chicken wire filled with dried sphagnum moss (see pages 24-25), which I bent into a circular shape and bound in wreath tape. I then wired large, overlapping bunches of wheat, lichen, and oregano onto the frame, and attached whole bulbs of garlic and decorative pomegranates, which had been dried and packed with newspaper, using a strong, fast-drying adhesive.

DRIED FLOWERS

UESTS WILL FREQUENTLY remark on the delicious fragrance as they enter a room filled with dried flowers. Their scents are quite heavenly, and they have a delicate charm and muted beauty that make them so appealing. Most flowers, even those that are not scented when they are fresh, have an aroma redolent of hay when they are dried. Roses, peonies, herbs, wattle, and mimosa retain their own distinctive scents and colors especially well. It is always best to keep all dried arrangements away from daylight, particularly direct sunlight, as the flowers will otherwise lose their color and brightness extremely quickly.

DRIED ROSE SWAG

This beautiful dried rose, hydrangea, and wattle swag would look quite magnificent seen hanging over a door or window, or adorning the top of a dresser or shelf. Dried flowers can be highly fragile, so I think it is usually best to make a dried swag using a rigid chicken-wire frame containing dried sphagnum moss (see pages 24-25), rather than a flexible rope or wire. Here, I used three frames to make three separate swags, and then tied the ends together to make a very colorful tripartite festoon.

37

CHRISTMAS WREATHS

FILL THE HOUSE with Christmas cheer by hanging a decorative wreath of flowers and foliage on the front door to welcome visitors. It is best to hang your wreath just a few days before Christmas day, so it retains its beauty throughout the whole of the festive season until Twelfth Night.

FRESH FLOWER WREATH

If there are no winter frosts, I often blend fresh flowers with traditional foliage in outdoor wreaths. Their bright colors and scents are a great delight in winter. Here, I have mixed 'Baccarola' roses with 'Jacaranda' roses and freesias. These nestle in clusters of berried skimmia foliage, against a dark background of evergreen Douglas fir.

INDEX

ACKNOWLEDGMENTS

The author would like to
thank Quentin Roake for all his help
in producing this book, and John Austin of
Covent Garden for supplying the flowers
that appeared in the book.

Dorling Kindersley would like
to thank Pauline Bayne, Polly Boyd,
Gill Della Casa, Jillian Haines,
Mary-Clare Jerram, and
Caroline Webber.